educate.ie

GW01090701

Fairground

Christmas Annual 2024

Author: Niall Callan

Illustrations: Emma Trithart/Bright Agency; Alex Patrick/Bright Agency

Recipe and craft testing and photography: Carla Gallagher

Design and layout: Liz White Designs

Cover design: Kieran O'Donoghue

Acknowledgements: Adobe Stock, Alamy, Shutterstock

ISBN: 978-1-916832-73-2

© 2024 Educate.ie

Printed in Ireland by Walsh Colour Print, Castleisland, Co. Kerry

Freephone 1800 613 111

Contents

Introduce Yourself

This Christmas annual belongs to

Name/Ainm/Imie/Ім'я:

Age/Aois/Wiek/Вік:

Class:

School:

Pauline Pinecone

Katie Sugarplum

Eddie Sparkles

Tina Tinsel

Billy Baubles

Old Red Curlytoes

CEANGAIL NA PONCANNA

Mandy an Miotán!

Ceangail na poncanna agus dathaigh an pictiúr.

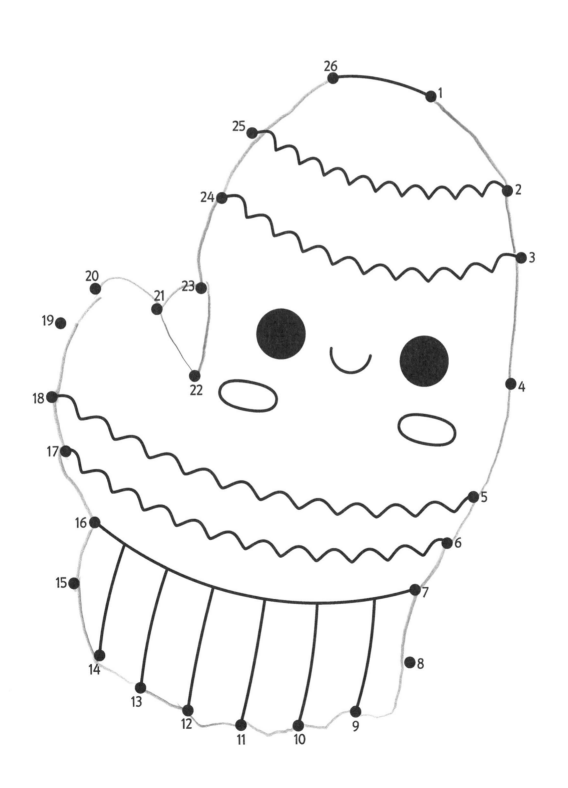

CROSSWORD

Can you solve this Christmas crossword?

Answers on page 78

6

DRAW AND COLOUR!

Copy the picture of the hedgehog, then colour it in.

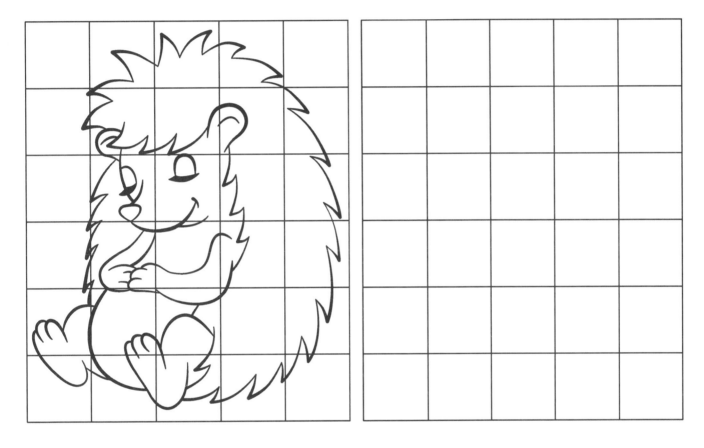

WORD SEARCH
Winter Walkies!

Throw on a warm jacket and take a walk through crisp snow in a winter forest. What do you see? Can you find any of these in the word search?

Holly **Spruce** **Mistletoe** **Ivy** **Berries**

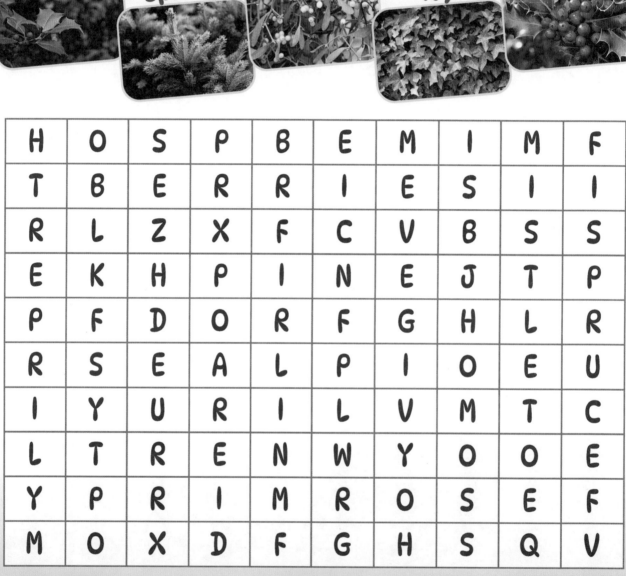

H	O	S	P	B	E	M	I	M	F
T	B	E	R	R	I	E	S	I	I
R	L	Z	X	F	C	V	B	S	S
E	K	H	P	I	N	E	J	T	P
P	F	D	O	R	F	G	H	L	R
R	S	E	A	L	P	I	O	E	U
I	Y	U	R	I	L	V	M	T	C
L	T	R	E	N	W	Y	O	O	E
Y	P	R	I	M	R	O	S	E	F
M	O	X	D	F	G	H	S	Q	V

Primrose **Pine** **Fern** **Fir** **Moss**

Answers on page 78

Puzzle It Out

What comes next? Draw your answer.

Answers on page 78

9

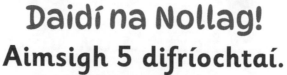

Daidí na Nollag!
Aimsigh 5 difríochtaí.

Freagraí ar leathanach 78

Recipe

ASK AN ADULT

Christmas Truffles

These super chocolatey treats are easy to make and decorate. You can use lots of different coatings to make them unique and they make a great Christmas present if you wrap them in a nice box or bag.

You will need:

150 g dark chocolate, chopped

150 g milk chocolate, chopped

150 ml cream

50 g unsalted butter

Flavourless oil (such as sunflower), for shaping

Different coatings: cocoa powder, sprinkles, edible glitter, icing sugar, chopped nuts

Small saucepan, whisk, bowl, teaspoon

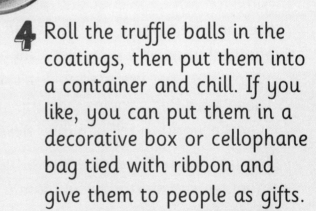

1 Put all the chocolate in a bowl, then put the cream and butter in a saucepan and heat them up, but make sure they do not boil.

2 Pour the hot cream over the chocolate and stir with a whisk until it melts. Leave to cool, then chill in the fridge for 6 hours, or overnight.

3 Put the coatings into separate bowls. To shape the truffles, lightly rub your hands with oil and roll teaspoons of the truffle mix between your palms to make balls. Watch out – this can get messy!

4 Roll the truffle balls in the coatings, then put them into a container and chill. If you like, you can put them in a decorative box or cellophane bag tied with ribbon and give them to people as gifts.

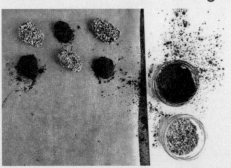

Truffles can be stored in the fridge in an airtight container for three days, or frozen for up to a month.

RED'S ROBINS

'Ready the Elf-o-plane! We've got a deep-cover mission on the books!' Katie Sugarplum called into her headset as she rushed about her North Pole office.

She'd been receiving worrying reports about a young boy in America, very worrying reports. She was hoping she'd be able to stop him from landing himself on the Naughty List before Christmas, even though there were only two months left until the big day. Before long, the elf pilots were busy running through checks in the cockpit, watching hundreds of flashing lights, pressing buttons and pulling levers.

Old Red Curlytoes shook his head as he watched the Elf-o-plane roar overhead, sitting on his favourite tree stump in the clearing in the forest where he lived.

'Time for work,' he chuckled, letting out a long musical whistle. Within seconds, he spied a flash of red in the trees, then another and another and another! After only a moment, all of the trees around him were covered in robins, their red breasts looking like giant holly berries on the branches. These were Red's robins, and they came to his North Pole home from all over the world to tell him their news.

The first robin flitted down from the tree, took up a perch on Old Red's shoulder and started tweeting and chirruping in his ear. Red listened along, occasionally interrupting with a question, an 'aha!' or an 'I see'. After each robin had finished its report, Old Red took out his Nice/Naughty Logbook and made a few notes beside the names of the children the robins had told him about. He worked late into the evening, listening to the robins and jotting down notes. Finally, it was the turn of Red's favourite robin, Bright Eyes, who had flown there all the way from Ireland. Bright Eyes settled on Red's shoulder and started tweeting away.

'Sounds like Ciara's being a great girl altogether,' muttered Red as Bright Eyes kept going. 'Maith thú, Kenzo! May be a bit of room for improvement there, Niall.'

Red continued to listen to Bright Eyes as she sang about all of the children she'd been keeping an eye on. After a while, her chirrups got louder and started to sound frantic.

'And which Emma is this?' asked Red, as the tweets continued, then, 'Oh yes, that one.'

Bright Eyes had told Red a lot about this particular Emma this year. She had just turned five and was in Junior Infants. Bright Eyes had perched on the windowsill of her classroom since September and had seen some things that had shocked her. One day, Emma had been tracing shapes in her handwriting copy and, all of a sudden, she got angry, ripped the page and threw the book on the floor.

Another day, when her teacher asked her to tidy up after Aistear, she had screamed 'NO!' at the teacher, ran into the play tent and refused to come out. After nearly an hour, her teacher had to call the principal! Bright Eyes couldn't understand why Old Red hadn't forwarded her file to Katie Sugarplum and the elf detectives. Of all the children she had seen, Emma should surely be on the Naughty List?

'Well, Bright Eyes, you see I've been doing this since before Eddie Sparkles had points on his ears, and there's more to this than meets the eye.' Bright Eyes cocked her head to one side, ready to hear more. 'Well, you're my best robin and you notice all the details, right? You told me that when Emma messed up the handwriting book, it was after her pencil had broken. And when she lost the plot at Aistear, it was because she was just about to finish a jigsaw she had been working on for ages. She's not *naughty*, Bright Eyes, she's *angry*.'

On hearing all of this, Bright Eyes let out a series of tweets, chirrups and whistles loud enough to frighten off some of the nearby robins.

'Oh, I know girl, it's not an excuse. Yes, she should have used her words on those occasions, but that's not so easy for some of us.' Bright Eyes cocked her head again and fixed Old Red with a quizzical stare. The old elf chuckled.

'You think I'm named Red because I look after you robins? Ha! I'm the oldest elf there is and there's no one left who remembers what I was like as a young'un, except for Santa of course. I was the angriest young elf there ever was! They called me Red because I would get so angry, I would see red ... and Curlytoes because they said I would rage so much that my toes would curl! When I'd get angry, I wouldn't be able to think or talk or do pretty much anything other than scream and shout!' Bright Eyes whistled slowly and softly.

'Yep,' said Red, 'I had to learn how to control all that. Sometimes I would just go outside and run. Sometimes I'd splash cold water on my face. Sometimes I would just need to take five.' Bright Eyes did her questioning head tilt again. 'Well that, my girl ... that's what we're going to teach Emma, together.'

A few days later, Emma was sitting in school doing some colouring. She put down the red crayon she was using and went to pick up the yellow, but it was gone! She noticed her neighbour Amira using it, and that made Emma ...

so ... ANGRY! She shot to her feet, knocking over her chair and was just about to scream when – TAPTAPTAPTAPTAP!

She looked up and saw a little robin tapping its beak on the classroom window. It distracted her for a second, but then she turned on Amira, opened her mouth and ... TAPTAPTAPTAPTAP! There was the robin again, tapping on the glass. As she watched it, the robin fluffed out the feathers on its chest again and again, *fluff, fluff, fluff, fluff, fluff.*

Five times. Emma found herself taking five deep breaths as she watched the robin, and with each breath a little bit of anger went away.

When her teacher came over to see what the matter was, she was still very angry, but she had calmed down enough to at least tell her about the crayon. Amira apologised. She hadn't realised that Emma was using it, so she gave it back and they both returned to their colouring.

The funny thing was, after that day, Emma kept seeing robins wherever she went! Any time she got angry and felt the red rage coming ... TAPTAPTAPTAPTAP! A robin

would tap on the window, or on a wall, or anything, and it would distract her. Then, as she watched it, it would do the feather trick, *fluff, fluff, fluff, fluff, fluff*, and she would find herself taking the five breaths. This calmed her down just enough to explain what was upsetting her to the teacher or one of her mammies. The more it happened, the calmer she would get, until one day, she found herself taking her five breaths even though no robin had appeared to interrupt her with a TAPTAPTAPTAPTAP!

In the week before Christmas, Old Red Curlytoes was grinning from ear to ear as Bright Eyes chortled and whistled a happy song in his ear.

'Good girl,' he said proudly.

Later that day, when he handed his Naughty/Nice Logbook to Katie Sugarplum, she frowned.

'You know, Red, you never give me anyone for the Naughty List, do you?'

'Nope,' he chuckled as he turned and headed back to the forest, 'I never do.'

Woolly Christmas Wreath

ASK AN ADULT

You will need:
Cardboard
Scissors
Green markers
Green wool
Tape
PVA glue
Buttons, sequins or gems
Ribbon

Create these woollen wreath decorations to add Christmas cheer to your home!

1 Trace two circles onto your cardboard, one bigger and one smaller, one inside the other. Cut out your wreath shape.

2 Next, colour the cardboard with a green marker so that if the wool doesn't cover the wreath shape completely, no one will notice! Tape one end of your wool to the back of the cardboard.

3 All that's left to do is wrap! Go around and around until the wreath shape is mostly covered.

4 Once it's covered, cut the wool and tape or glue the end to the back.

5 Use PVA glue to stick buttons, gemstones or sequins on to your wreath to decorate it.

6 Take a piece of ribbon and tie it to the wreath for hanging!

JOIN THE DOTS

All Spruced Up!

Join the dots and colour the picture!

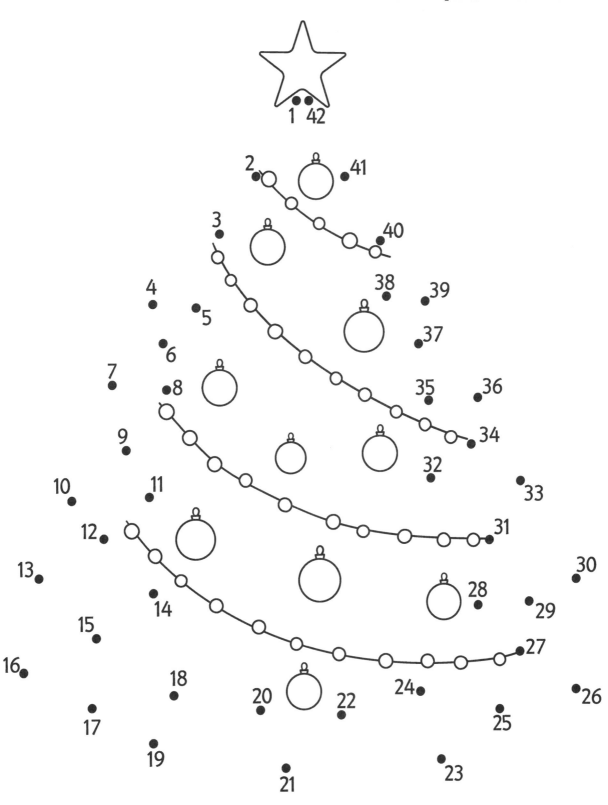

CROSSWORD

Can you fill in the names of our winter friends?

Answers on page 78

WORD SEARCH
The Arctic Circle

The Arctic Circle covers a large area.
Lots of countries (and Santa's North Pole
Village) have areas inside the Arctic Circle.
Can you find them in the word search?

Russia

Norway

Finland

Greenland

S	P	A	F	R	A	D	A	M	F	S
S	W	E	D	E	N	D	L	E	Z	M
G	L	A	X	A	E	V	L	L	D	G
E	E	P	L	B	D	O	K	D	N	R
R	O	E	B	L	P	X	A	R	A	E
L	C	A	C	H	P	E	T	E	L	E
I	Y	A	T	T	E	N	I	D	N	N
N	T	R	R	U	S	S	I	A	I	L
E	O	I	B	S	R	G	I	M	F	A
N	O	R	W	A	Y	A	M	F	V	N
L	I	A	F	C	A	N	A	D	A	D

Canada

Iceland

Sweden

USA

North Pole

Answers on page 78

Claude Monet

Winter is a great time of year to draw, paint and do all sorts of art. There are lots of interesting things to look at: the bright colours of a Christmas tree, or the quieter, more peaceful colours of a snowy day. One artist who loved to paint both bright and quiet pictures was the painter Claude Monet. Monet  was born in France on 14 November 1840, and he grew up to become one of the most famous artists in the world.

Monet loved to paint the beautiful scenes he saw around him, from colourful gardens to shimmering water lilies. One of Monet's favourite things to paint was winter. *The Magpie* is one of his most famous winter paintings. In this painting, he drew a lone magpie perched on a gatepost in the middle of a snowy field. The magpie's black and white feathers stand out against the snowy white landscape. Another famous winter painting by Monet is called *Snow at Argenteuil*. In this painting, he shows the quiet of a snowy day in a town near Paris.

Monet's winter paintings were loved by people all around the world. They were amazed by the way he could capture the magic of winter on canvas and bring it to life with his paintbrush.

Think back on what you have read ...

1 Where was Claude Monet from?

2 When was he born?

3 Can you name one of Claude Monet's famous winter paintings?

4 What other things did he like to paint?

Tell us what you think ...

Do you think winter is beautiful? Why?

_____

_____

_____

Figure It Out!

How many of each can you find?
Write your answer in the box!

one	two	three	four	five
six	seven	eight	nine	ten

| three | 3 | 7 | 4 | 4 |

Answers on page 78

22

SUDOKU

Which robins and presents belong in the missing squares? Each picture should appear only once in each line – up and down AND side to side!

Answers on page **78**

SPOT THE DIFFERENCE

Is the Easter Bunny Lost?!
Can you spot 8 differences?

Answers on page 78

Fíor nó Bréagach

Más fíor, cuir ✔ sa bhosca.
Más bréagach, cuir ✗ sa bhosca.

 Tá sé ag imirt peile.

 Tá sé ag léamh.

 Tá sé ag scríobh.

 Tá siad ag damhsa.

 Tá sé ag léim.

Freagraí ar leathanach 78

Is féidir liom _____ .

25

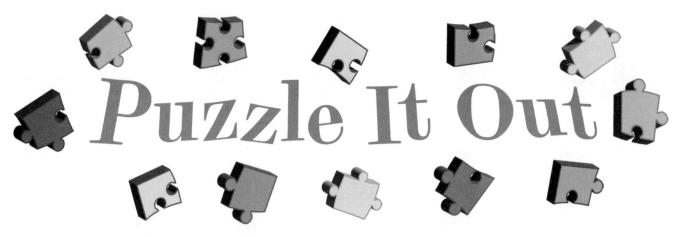

Puzzle It Out

Find the way from each decoration to the Christmas tree!

Answers on page 78

Figure It Out!

Can you solve these word problems?

Katie Sugarplum spends 3 hours working on the Nice List on Monday, 2 hours working on it on Tuesday and 4 hours working on it on Wednesday.

How long did it take her to write it?

Old Red Curlytoes was looking at 11 of his robins sitting on a branch. 5 of them flew away.

How many are left?

Santa went down the chimneys of 21 houses on one side of a street and 21 houses on the other side.

How many houses were there on the street?

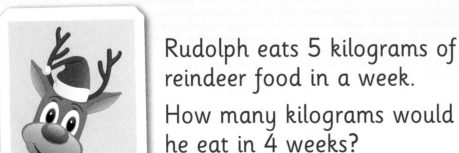

Rudolph eats 5 kilograms of reindeer food in a week.

How many kilograms would he eat in 4 weeks?

Answers on page 78

Only Joking!

How does a snowman get around?

By riding an "icicle"!

What do you call an elf who sings?

A wrapper!

Why was the snowman looking through the carrots?

He was picking his nose!

How do snowmen greet each other?

Ice to meet you!

Why don't polar bears like fast food?

Because they can't catch it!

Why did the gingerbread man go to the doctor?

He was feeling crumbly!

What do elves use to wrap presents?

Elf-adhesive tape!

What do you get when you cross a snowman and a baker?

Frosting!

What do you call a snowman with a six-pack?

An abdominal snowman!

Why don't snowmen ever get into fights?

They're too 'chilled' out!

What's Santa's favourite type of pizza?

One that's 'deep pan, crisp, and even'!

Why was the turkey in the pop group?

Because it had the drumsticks!

What's the favourite Christmas carol of parents?

Silent Night!

What's green, covered in tinsel, and goes 'ribbit, ribbit'?

A mistle-toad!

Why was the Christmas tree not feeling well?

It had tinsel-itis!

What did the stamp say to the Christmas card?

Stick with me, and we'll go places!

FACTS!

Did you know ...?

The song 'Jingle Bells' was originally written for the American holiday of Thanksgiving, not Christmas.

The tradition of hanging stockings by the fireplace comes from a legend about Saint Nicholas, who dropped gold coins down a chimney.

The tallest Christmas tree ever displayed was over 67 metres tall and was erected in a Washington shopping mall in 1950.

The tradition of hanging ornaments on Christmas trees started in Germany in the 16th century.

In some parts of Ukraine, it's traditional to decorate Christmas trees with artificial spiders and webs.

In Italy, it's traditional to eat a meal of seven different kinds of fish on Christmas Eve.

Candy canes were originally created in Germany in the 17th century and were straight, not curved.

The world's largest gathering of Santa Clauses took place in Ireland in 2007, with 13,000 Santas.

In Germany, it's traditional to hide a pickle ornament in the Christmas tree, and the first child to find it gets an extra present.

The first artificial Christmas trees were made in Germany out of dyed goose feathers.

The tradition of sending Christmas cards began in England in 1843.

In Norway, it's traditional to hide all the brooms in the house on Christmas Eve to prevent witches and evil spirits from stealing them.

The tradition of the yule log dates back to ancient times when people would burn large logs to ward off evil spirits during the winter solstice.

In Poland, it's traditional to place hay under the tablecloth at Christmas dinner to symbolise the manger where Jesus was born.

The world's largest Christmas cracker was made in the UK in 2001 and measured almost 64 metres long.

MAP OF IRELAND

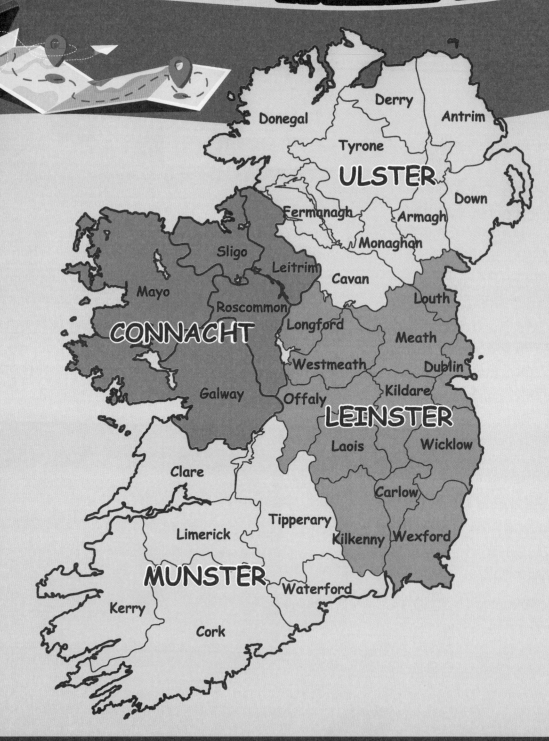

- Put a circle around the county that you live in.
- Find Dublin and draw a star in it.
- Find Cork and draw a triangle in it.
- Draw a smiley face in Donegal.
- Draw a wavy line in Mayo.
- Tick off any counties you have visited.

Puzzle It Out

What can you see in the jumbled picture? Draw your answers in the boxes below!

ASK AN ADULT

Billy Baubles' Favourite Doughnuts

Billy Baubles loves nothing more after a hard day's work than to sit back with a cup of cocoa and an elf doughnut. They're much smaller than your usual doughnut, so watch out you don't eat too many!

You will need:

2 tbsp melted butter, plus an extra 1 tbsp for greasing

100 g plain flour

1/2 tsp baking powder

1 tsp ground cinnamon

1/4 tsp ground nutmeg

3 tbsp caster sugar

1 large egg

1 tsp vanilla extract

2 tbsp honey or maple syrup

4 tbsp buttermilk

For the icing:

250 g icing sugar

50 ml milk

Red and green food colouring

Sprinkles

Mini muffin tin, pastry brush, large bowl, bowl or jug, fork or whisk, wooden spoon, two teaspoons, apple corer

1 Preheat the oven to 180° C/ 160° C fan/gas mark 4. Brush some melted butter in the holes of a 24-hole mini muffin tin.

2 Mix the flour, baking powder, cinnamon, nutmeg and sugar in a big bowl.

3 Pour the melted butter into a bowl or jug with the egg, vanilla, honey/maple syrup and buttermilk, and mix together with a whisk or fork.

4 Mix the wet and dry ingredients together with a spoon, making sure you don't leave any lumps.

5 Use two teaspoons to divide the mixture between the holes in the tin and bake for 8–10 mins, then cool in the tin.

6 When they have cooled, transfer the little cakes to a chopping board and push an apple corer into the centre to cut the middle out so you have a doughnut shape.

7 Whisk the icing sugar and milk until you have a smooth icing. You can choose to leave it white as snow, or you can divide the mixture between a few bowls and use some food colouring for a more festive look.

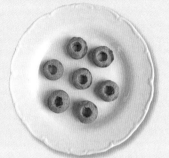

8 Sit the doughnuts on a wire rack (so the drips can fall off), then spoon a little icing onto each. Decorate with sprinkles if you like.

The doughnuts will keep fresh in an airtight container for two days.

35

Meaitseáil

An Fear Sneachta

Tarraing líne idir an bpictiúr agus an focal.

1 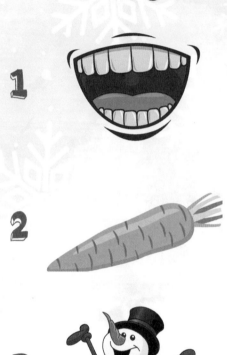 → súile

2 srón

3 béal

4 cairéad

5 fear sneachta

Féach ar an fear sneachta.

Freagraí ar leathanach 79

SPOT THE DIFFERENCE

All Aboard the Toy Train!
Can you find the 10 differences?

Answers on page 79

North Pole

What sorts of buildings are there in Santa's North Pole village? There's the Frozen Grill where the elves like to relax with a Chillyburger after work.

Village

There's the reindeer stables and toy production factory, but what else? Use your imagination to draw your own North Pole village on these pages.

Jingle Bell Mini Wreath

ASK AN ADULT

You will need:
Wire
Scissors
Greenery such as ivy, pine twigs and holly
Jingle bells (you can buy them online, from a craft shop or pet shop)
Ribbon

Fill your home with the sound of jingling bells this Christmas with this lovely ornament!

1 Bend some wire into a small circle.

2 Wrap the greenery around the wire and secure it in place with more wire if necessary.

5 Finally, tie a large bow to the mini wreath.

3 Thread the jingle bells onto some lengths of ribbon and tie them to the mini wreath.

4 You may need to tie some knots in the ribbon to secure the bells in place.

Dathaigh na hUimhreacha

Tá teidí istigh sa stoca.

 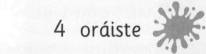

HELP SANTA!

Can you help Santa visit all of the houses? You will need a dice and some counters. If you like, you can use small toys!

- Landing on an orange circle means you can skip forward, but a red one will bring you back!

- If you land on number 13, go back to the start.

- Move forward three spaces if you land on a present or festive treat.

- If you land on number 33 or reach the finish line first, you win!

START · 1 · 3 · 2 · 28 · 2 · 36 · 37 · 39 · 40 · 42 · 43 · 44 · 45 · 46 · 35 · 34

Puzzle It Out

What comes next?
Circle the correct item for each empty box.

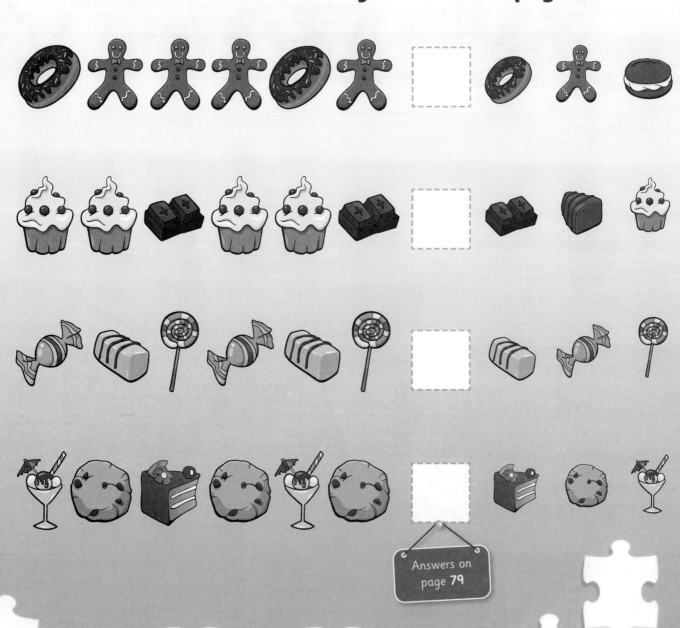

Answers on page 79

44

CROSSWORD
Guess Who?

Answers on page 79

JOIN THE DOTS

Peter Penguin!

Join the dots and colour the picture!

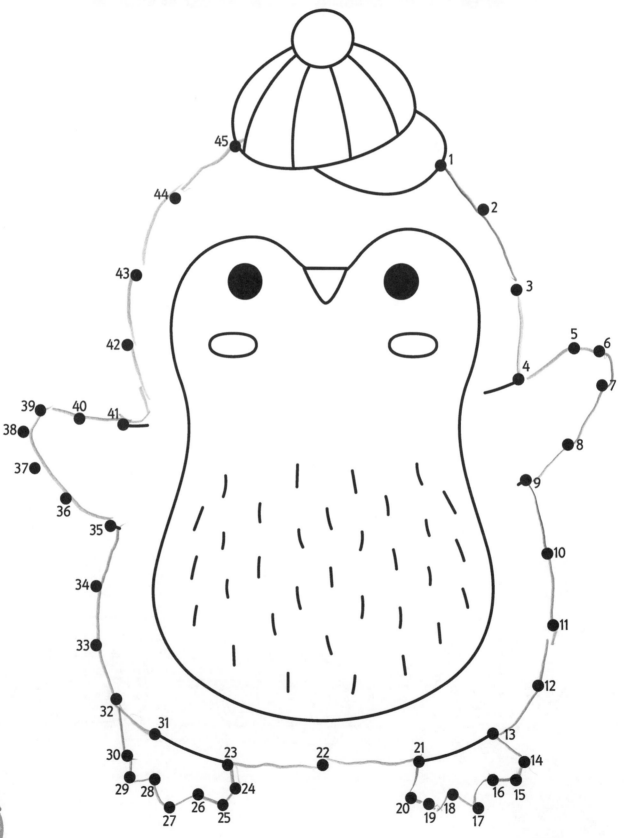

Puzzle It Out

Eddie Sparkles is sorting his smelly socks to put them in the washing machine. Find the odd one out, then colour the picture!

Answers on page **79**

Charles Dickens

Christmas is a great time for stories and there are lots of wonderful tales we think of around this time. One of the most famous Christmas stories was written by Charles Dickens, an English writer who lived over 200 years ago.

Charles Dickens was born on 7 February 1812 in Portsmouth, England. He was the second of eight children in his family. When Charles was young, his family didn't have much money, and he had to leave school at a young age to work.

As he grew older, Charles became a journalist and began writing novels. One of his most famous books is called *A Christmas Carol*. This story was written in 1843, and it's all about the magic of Christmas and the power of kindness and generosity.

A Christmas Carol tells the story of a grumpy old man named Ebenezer Scrooge. Scrooge has lots of money but is mean and stingy, and he doesn't like Christmas at all. One Christmas Eve, Scrooge is visited by three ghosts who show Scrooge his past, present and future, and they teach him important lessons about kindness, compassion and the true meaning of Christmas.

By the end of the story, Scrooge has transformed into a kind and generous man who loves Christmas and cares for others.

Charles Dickens wrote many other wonderful books and stories during his lifetime, but *A Christmas Carol* remains one of his best-loved books and has been made into TV shows and movies, even one including the Muppets!

Think back on the story ...

1 Who was Charles Dickens, and where was he from?

2 What was one of Charles Dickens' most famous books, and what is it about?

3 Describe the character Ebenezer Scrooge. What was he like?

4 What lessons does Scrooge learn in *A Christmas Carol*?

Tell us what you think ...

If you were to write a famous Christmas story, what would it be about?

My story would be about:

_____

_____

_____

Meaitseáil

Bia Blasta

Tarraing líne idir an bpictiúr agus an focal.

1    milseáin

2    cáca milis

3    criospaí

4 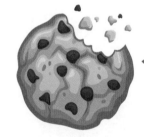   brioscaí

5     uachtar reoite

Freagraí ar leathanach 79

Is maith liom _____.

COLOURING

Tina Tinsel, one of Santa's most hard-working elves, loves to paint Christmas tree baubles in her spare time. Can you help her complete these?

CODE BREAKER

Crack the code to reveal the Christmas songs.

A	B	C	D	E	F	G	H	I	J	K	L	M
1	2	3	4	5	6	7	8	9	10	11	12	13

N	O	P	Q	R	S	T	U	V	W	X	Y	Z
14	15	16	17	18	19	20	21	22	23	24	25	26

1

12	5	20

9	20

19	14	15	23

2

19	9	12	5	14	20

14	9	7	8	20

3

13	5	18	18	25

3	8	18	9	19	20	13	1	19

5	22	5	18	25	15	14	5

Answers on page 79

SUDOKU

Which Christmas animal friends belong in the missing squares?

Each picture should appear only once in each line – up and down AND side to side!

Answers on page 79

All I Want for Christmas

Read with me

IT WAS THE FIRST WEEK IN DECEMBER and Mr O'Brien's Second Class was buzzing with excitement. Mr O'Brien had a rule that the 'C' word couldn't be mentioned in his classroom in November, but once December began he went crazy for Christmas, letting the boys and girls make decorations and do lots of Christmas art, and even making the children hot chocolate with marshmallows when they were really good!

Today they were using their English lesson to write letters to Santa. As the teacher walked around the classroom checking on handwriting and helping with spellings, he noticed a sad face sticking out among all of the happy ones.

'You don't look too happy, Jack,' he said, leaning down so he could have a private chat with the little boy. 'What's the matter?'

'Nothing!' said Jack sharply, but Mr O'Brien could tell that wasn't true. He decided to give Jack some time to take a breath and just before home time, he asked him again.

'Well,' said a slightly calmer Jack, 'It's embarrassing and you'll probably think it's weird, but I really, really want this doll for Christmas. I saw her in a shop last weekend and she's so beautiful. She has funky blue hair and really cool outfits and loads of accessories and she's basically the only thing I want – if I could have her, I wouldn't want anything else!'

'Okay,' replied Mr O'Brien, 'I don't see why that'd be weird or embarrassing. Why were you upset? Do you think the doll will be too expensive or something?'

'No,' sighed Jack, 'but my brother said I couldn't ask for a doll. He said everyone would make fun of me and that boys shouldn't play with dolls, they're just for girls! He said people would call me weird and say I was a girl and I'm NOT a girl, I'm a BOY!' With that, Jack began to get very upset again and before Mr O'Brien could say anything to help, his mam arrived, and he ran across the playground to meet her.

The next day was Friday and Mr O'Brien saw Jack trudge into school looking very sad. He didn't put up his hand to answer questions, he stayed by himself in the yard, and at the end of the day during Golden Time he stayed at his table reading alone while the others played board games. Mr O'Brien took something

out of his bag, walked over and sat down beside Jack. 'I was thinking about what you told me yesterday, Jack,' he said. 'And I brought this in from home to show you. Did you know I used to play with dolls when I was your age?'

Jack's head shot up, stunned. 'Really?' he asked, as Mr O'Brien handed over what he'd been carrying. Jack's face instantly fell. It was an old army figure with a grizzled expression on his face, a camouflage jumpsuit and a toy rifle in his hand. 'That's not a doll, Teacher. It's an Action Man.'

Mr O'Brien smiled and shook his head. 'It's a doll, Jack. It's plastic, it has moveable arms and legs, it's virtually the exact same size as the doll you'd like.

'And when I was your age, I loved putting him in imaginary situations, and I was obsessed with getting all the different clothes and accessories I could for him, just like you'll be with your doll. The only difference is that my doll was male and the one you want is female.'

'No, Teacher. It's totally different! I bet no one made fun of you for playing with him!'

'You're right Jack, no one did. But no one in this class will make fun of you for playing with your doll. I can guarantee you that. And if you'd like, I can have a word with your mother and make sure no one at home makes fun of your doll either.' Mr O'Brien got up to go back to his desk, put a kind hand on Jack's shoulder and said, 'You should ask Santa for the toy you want, Jack.'

Ten minutes later, Mr O'Brien looked up from his desk where he was correcting copies. Jack's hand was up. 'Yes, Jack?' he asked.

'Teacher, can I have a sheet of paper to write on please?' replied Jack, with a smile.

Puzzle It Out

Can you help our North Pole friends find their presents under the tree?

Answers on page 79

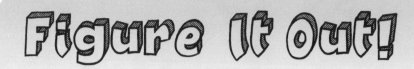

Figure It Out!

Can you solve these word problems?

Sleety the snowman is collecting clothes for the new snowmen in his village. If there are 12 new snowmen, how many gloves will he need?

Every time it snows, Seán the snowman grows a bit taller! If 3 cm of snow fell on Monday, 4 cm of snow fell on Tuesday, and 5 cm of snow fell on Wednesday, how much taller is he now all together?

The snowmen are getting ready for their five-a-side soccer tournament. If there are 20 snowmen, and 5 snowmen go on each team, how many teams can be made?

Frosty the snowman decided he wanted a makeover. He bought a new hat for €5, a scarf for €6, gloves for €7 and a new carrot for €1. How much money did he spend?

Answers on page 80

WORD SEARCH

Yummy Christmas!

candy cane

chocolate

Ham

Mince pies

Y	M	R	Y	U	M	S	L	H	T	G	N	D	L	M	B	U	L
P	J	L	O	I	G	M	T	A	G	T	A	R	L	F	Q	C	L
O	T	S	Z	D	C	R	I	M	T	X	U	Z	I	J	I	A	W
T	T	V	T	P	D	H	H	N	G	G	F	R	G	H	P	N	J
A	T	E	A	U	P	X	O	D	C	H	T	I	K	V	U	D	K
T	R	A	R	W	F	U	T	C	X	E	O	V	X	E	P	Y	L
O	M	J	H	F	P	F	D	Z	O	A	P	C	Y	I	Y	C	U
E	A	Y	N	Q	P	K	I	D	X	L	Y	I	M	F	W	A	Y
S	X	T	N	W	A	A	C	N	I	Z	A	Y	E	T	W	N	V
G	T	Y	W	U	A	F	V	G	G	N	B	T	X	S	L	E	Q
N	G	W	W	T	U	D	Z	P	C	O	G	V	E	T	L	Z	L
A	F	B	Z	G	O	H	B	K	W	M	Z	E	I	N	G	H	L

potatoes

Pudding

Stuffing

Turkey

Answers on page 80

59

ELF OFF THE SHELF

It was close to Christmas and on the toy shelf,
Everyone was sleeping, except one silly Elf!
Every night he'd get up and he'd mess around,
Using the slinky to climb down to the ground.

Once he was down; oh, the things that he did!
Everything adults would usually forbid!
He unrolled the toilet paper all over the floor,
Put Sellotape all round the edge of the door!
Filled the freezer with snowballs and let food go to waste,
Wrote all over the mirror with minty toothpaste!

He put forks in the fridge and poured milk in the drawer,
There was mischief and messing and much worse and more!

Other toys asked him to mend his bad ways,
So he took Barbie hostage and locked Ken up for days.
He wouldn't listen, not even to old Teddy Bear,
The rules didn't matter, he just didn't care!

Because every morning, what the others didn't see,
Was the laughter and smiles and happiness and glee.
All of the antics of this terrible, bold toy,
Brought the children who owned him nothing but joy.

60

Fíor nó Bréagach

Más fíor, cuir ✔ sa bhosca.

Más bréagach, cuir ✘ sa bhosca.

 Is breá liom burgar. ☐

 Is breá liom ispíní. ☐

 Is breá liom sceallóga. ☐

 Is breá liom píotsa. ☐

 Is breá liom pasta. ☐

Is fearr liom _____.

CÉ MHÉAD?

Cé mhéad de gach rud atá sa phictiúr?
Scríobh an uimhir sa bhosca.

1 = amháin	2 = dhá	3 = trí	4 = ceithre	5 = cúig

amháin

Freagraí ar leathanach 80

JOIN THE DOTS

Blingy Baubles!

Join the dots and colour the picture!

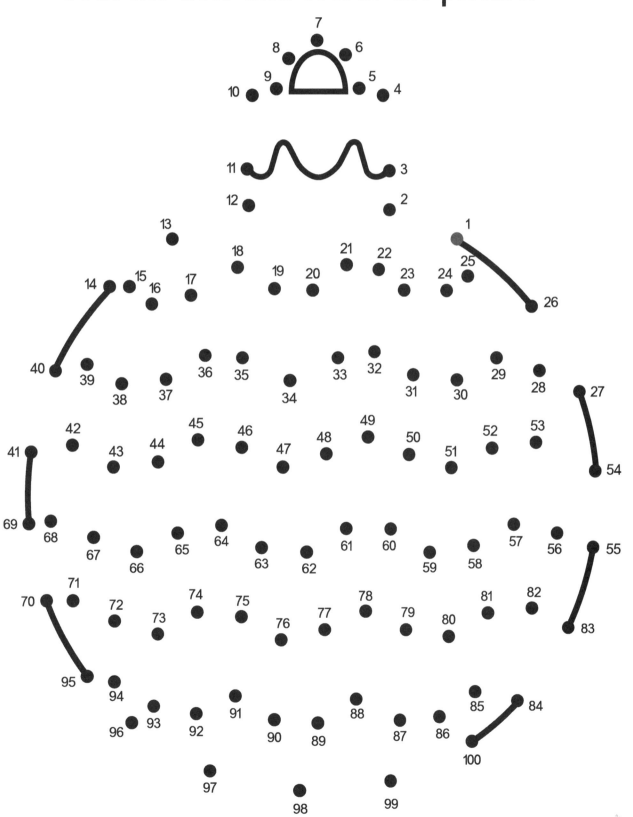

La Flor de Nochebuena

Lots of people like to decorate their houses with red flowers called poinsettias at Christmas. The custom was introduced in the United States by a man called Joel Poinsett in the 1820s, but he got the idea from travelling to Mexico, where people had been using these flowers as decorations for much longer. Here's the story of why ...

ONCE UPON A TIME IN MEXICO, there was a young girl named Pepita. In Pepita's village, people presented gifts to a statue of the baby Jesus in the church on Christmas Eve. Pepita's family didn't have much money and she was sad that she would have no gift to bring. Pepita's cousin, Pedro, tried to comfort her, reminding her that even the smallest gift is important if it is given with love.

As Pepita and Pedro made their way to the church, Pedro encouraged Pepita to pick some weeds by the roadside to offer as her gift. Pepita wasn't sure, feeling embarrassed to be bringing weeds, but Pedro assured her that it was the thought and love behind the gift that mattered most.

As they entered the church, Pepita placed the bundle of weeds at the foot of the nativity scene. Suddenly, the weeds burst into beautiful red and green star-shaped flowers! Everyone in the church was amazed by this miraculous transformation.

From that day on, the red and green flowers, which came to be known as poinsettias, became a symbol of Christmas in Mexico. The story of the Christmas Eve flower – 'la flor de Nochebuena' – reminds people of the importance of giving from the heart, no matter how small the gift may seem.

Think about it ...

If you had no money to buy a gift, what would you make or bring?

The gift I would give would be _____ because:

_____

_____

Colour the poinsettia below!

Meaitseáil

Eadaí Deasa

Tarraing líne idir an bpictiúr agus an focal.

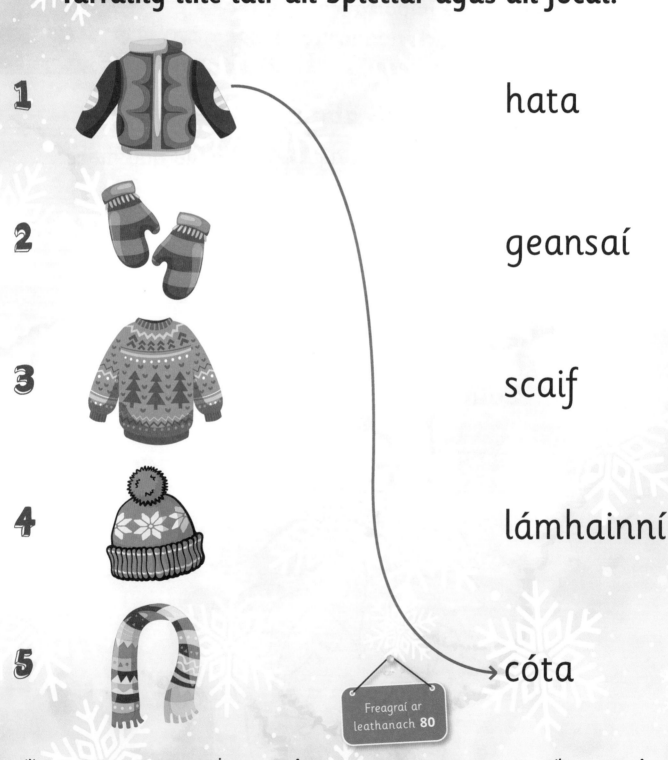

1   hata

2   geansaí

3   scaif

4   lámhainní

5   cóta

Freagraí ar leathanach 80

Cuir ort do chóta, tá sé fuar!

Draw!

Copy these steps to draw your own reindeer!

① ② ③ ④ ⑤

MISTLETOE KISSES!

OVER A THOUSAND YEARS AGO, the Vikings lived in Denmark, Sweden, Norway and Finland. They voyaged around Europe, sometimes getting into battles and stealing treasure, and sometimes trading and making new homes. Many Vikings visited Ireland and came to live here, founding towns and cities like Wexford, Waterford, Limerick, Cork and Dublin.

Read with me

The Vikings loved to tell stories and had many myths about their gods and goddesses. One of their myths explains why people like to kiss under the mistletoe.

Long ago, in the land of the Vikings, there was a goddess named Frigg. She had a son named Baldur, who was very special because he brought light and happiness to everyone.

Frigg loved Baldur very much and wanted to protect him from harm. So, she asked every plant and animal in the world to promise not to hurt him. But there was one plant she didn't ask: mistletoe. Mistletoe seemed too tiny and harmless to worry about.

Frigg

Baldur

But the trickster god Loki saw this as a chance to cause trouble. He made a spear out of mistletoe and tricked Baldur's blind brother, Hodur, into throwing it at Baldur during a game. Sadly, Baldur was killed, and Frigg and Hodur were heartbroken.

Loki

But then something wonderful happened! All of the other gods worked together to bring him back to life. Frigg was overjoyed and decided that mistletoe would no longer be a symbol of sadness. Instead, she said it would be a symbol of love and friendship.

From that day on, whenever people found mistletoe hanging, they would give each other kisses underneath it to show love, friendship and forgiveness. And that's why we still kiss under mistletoe at Christmastime today!

Think about it ...

Can you make up your own creative, or even silly, reason why people choose to kiss under this strange-looking plant?

I think people like to kiss under the mistletoe because:

_____

_____

Use the space here to draw a picture of your favourite god from the story: Baldur, Frigg, Loki or Hodur!

WORD SEARCH

Santa's Stables

Can you find the names of all of the reindeer in Santa's stables?

Dasher   Dancer   Vixen   Rudolph

Donner   Comet   Prancer

Blitzen   Cupid

N	N	M	G	O	P	E	B	W	M	S	S	P	O	L	E	J	D
R	K	Z	V	I	X	E	N	D	I	H	C	L	C	X	N	Z	P
B	L	I	T	Z	E	N	H	A	P	T	L	I	C	T	O	N	H
Q	M	A	V	D	R	R	D	S	H	R	L	L	Q	O	Q	C	T
D	U	Z	J	O	U	K	N	H	X	N	A	O	Y	O	K	G	B
U	H	C	M	N	D	D	I	E	L	A	L	N	L	H	I	O	Y
B	R	L	O	N	O	C	U	R	C	G	R	W	C	M	R	Z	M
R	W	B	I	E	L	C	O	M	E	T	F	I	N	E	U	N	W
C	M	O	G	R	P	X	B	Q	K	J	T	K	U	L	R	Q	J
K	S	H	L	S	H	H	M	C	U	P	I	D	Z	O	N	E	X
L	O	H	X	E	M	L	J	O	O	G	I	T	D	P	V	U	Q
L	M	C	P	D	A	N	C	E	R	S	C	W	G	P	A	X	Z

Answers on
page 80

70

Shhhhhhh

Falling snow doesn't make any sound,
You could almost say it's a whisper,
Telling the world to quiet down.
It tumbles from the sky in silent sheets,
Pillowy mounds softly blanket the ground,
Lulling the world to sleep.

Jack Frost's Chocolate Bark

You will need:
300 g white chocolate
Blue food colouring gel
Blue/silver sprinkles, stars, balls
Two bowls, a baking sheet, baking paper, cocktail sticks

This chocolate bark is fun to make and swirling the colours together feels like a science experiment! We used white and blue for a winter look, but you can use any colour you want.

1 Line a baking sheet with baking paper.

2 Melt the chocolate in a bowl set over a pan of simmering water or in the microwave.

3 Put one third of the melted chocolate into another bowl and add a tiny amount of blue food colouring. Mix it in. Add a few drops at a time until you have a pale blue colour. (If the chocolate clumps up, add tiny amounts of boiling water and stir until it looks smooth and glossy again.)

4 Pour the uncoloured white chocolate onto the lined sheet. Spread it around a bit. Add little blobs of the blue chocolate all over the white chocolate. Use cocktail sticks to swirl the chocolate together until you have a lovely marbled pattern.

5 Add the edible decorations and leave to chill in the fridge until solid.

Break into pieces and enjoy, or put pieces into small bags to give as presents.

SUDOKU

Have you tried the sudoku puzzles on pages 23 and 53? Try this one using the numbers 1, 2, 3 and 4!

Can you figure out the missing numbers?

Each number should appear only once in each small square, and once in each line — up and down AND side to side!

TIP!

Try to figure out which numbers are missing, then you can try to work out where they might go. If you get stuck, try a different row or square!

		3	
3	2		4
		4	1
1	4		

Now try this one, using numbers 5, 6, 7 and 8!

6			7
		8	
	6		5
7		6	

Answers on page 80

Figure It Out!

Can you solve these word problems?

If Annabel buys a hot chocolate for €2 and asks for cream to be added for an extra 50c and marshmallows to be added for an extra 40c, how much will it all cost?

Kuba wants to buy some Christmas cookies to take away for himself, his mam, his dad and his sister Olivia. If the cookies cost €1.50 each, how much will he have to spend?

Amina wants to buy a snowman cupcake for €2. How much change will she get if she pays with a €10 note?

Mary's nana shared €20 equally between Mary, her brothers Paddy and Thomas, and her sister Katie. How much money did each child get?

Answers on page 80

Puzzle It Out

Can you find the hidden objects in this picture?

Answers on page 80

Checklist

You're nearly at the end of this year's *Fairground* annual! Well done!

Time to tick ✓ off your checklist.

Have you ...

Learned about an artist you never knew before? ☐

Tried out a recipe? ☐

Finished a sudoku? ☐

Coloured a picture? ☐

Completed a word search? ☐

Relaxed with a lovely Christmas story? ☐

Been creative with arts and crafts? ☐

Great work! Now there's one last thing to do ...

CoLouring

HAPPY NEW YEAR!

2025

ANSWERS/FREAGRAÍ

Page 6 Crossword

1. SNOWGLOBE
2. DEER
3. PRESENT
4. SNOWMAN
5. STOCKING
6. SANTA

Page 10 Aimsigh na Difríochtaí

Page 23 Sudoku

Page 8 Word Search

H	O	S	P	B	E	M	I	M	F
T	B	E	R	R	I	E	S	I	I
R	L	Z	X	F	C	V	B	S	S
E	K	H	P	I	N	E	J	T	P
P	F	D	O	R	F	G	H	L	R
R	S	E	A	L	P	I	O	E	U
I	Y	U	R	I	L	V	M	T	C
L	T	R	E	N	W	Y	O	O	E
Y	P	R	I	M	R	O	S	E	F
M	O	X	D	F	G	H	S	Q	V

Page 18 Crossword

1. BEAR
2. PENGUIN
3. DEER
4. OWL
5. WALRUS
6. CROSS / RABBIT
7. SNOWMAN / SANTA

Page 24 Spot the Difference

Page 9 Puzzle It Out

Page 19 Word Search

S	P	A	F	R	A	D	A	M	F	S
S	W	E	D	E	N	D	L	E	Z	M
G	L	A	X	A	E	V	L	L	D	G
E	E	P	L	B	D	O	K	D	N	R
R	O	E	B	L	P	X	A	R	A	E
L	C	A	C	H	P	E	T	E	L	E
I	Y	A	T	T	E	N	I	D	N	N
N	T	R	R	U	S	S	I	A	I	L
E	O	I	B	S	R	G	I	M	F	A
N	O	R	W	A	Y	A	M	F	V	N
L	I	A	F	C	A	N	A	D	A	D

Page 22 Figure It Out!

| three | three | seven | five | four |

Page 25 Fíor nó Bréagach

Tá sé ag imirt peile. ✗
Tá sé ag léamh. ✓
Tá sé ag scríobh. ✗
Tá siad ag damhsa. ✓
Tá sé ag léim. ✗

Page 26 Puzzle It Out

Page 27 Figure It Out!
9 hours, 6 robins, 42 houses, 20 kilograms

Page 36 Meaitseáil

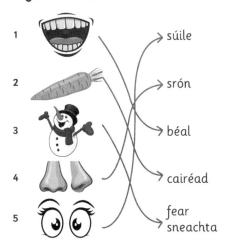

1 → súile

2 → srón

3 → béal

4 → cairéad

5 → fear sneachta

Page 37 Spot the Difference

Page 44 Puzzle It Out

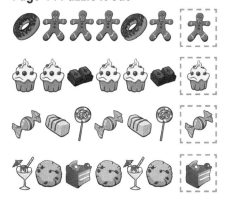

Page 45 Crossword

Page 47 Puzzle It Out

10 (1–4, 2–9, 3–7, 5–11, 6–8)

Page 50 Meaitseáil

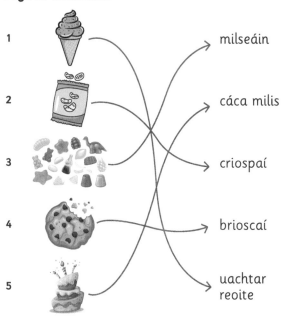

1 → milseáin

2 → cáca milis

3 → criospaí

4 → brioscaí

5 → uachtar reoite

Page 52 Code Breaker

1. Let it Snow, 2. Silent Night,
3. Merry Christmas Everyone

Page 53 Sudoku

Page 57 Puzzle It Out

Page 58 Figure It Out!

24 gloves (12 pairs), 12 centimetres, 4 teams, €19

Page 59 Word Search

Y	M	R	Y	U	M	S	L	H	T	G	N	D	L	M	B	U	L
P	J	L	O	I	G	M	T	A	G	T	A	R	L	F	Q	C	L
O	T	S	Z	D	C	R	I	M	T	X	U	Z	I	J	I	A	W
T	T	V	T	P	D	H	H	N	G	G	F	R	G	H	P	N	J
A	T	E	A	U	P	X	O	D	C	H	T	I	K	V	U	D	K
T	R	A	R	W	F	U	T	C	X	E	O	V	X	E	P	Y	L
O	M	J	H	F	P	F	D	Z	O	A	P	C	Y	I	Y	C	U
E	A	Y	N	Q	P	K	I	D	X	L	Y	I	M	F	W	A	Y
S	X	T	N	W	A	A	C	N	I	Z	A	Y	E	T	W	N	V
G	T	Y	W	U	A	F	V	G	G	N	B	T	X	S	L	E	Q
N	G	W	W	T	U	D	Z	P	C	O	G	V	E	T	L	Z	L
A	F	B	Z	G	O	H	B	K	W	M	Z	E	I	N	G	H	L

Page 62 Cé Mhéad?

amháin

cúig

dhá

ceithre

trí

Page 66 Meaitseáil

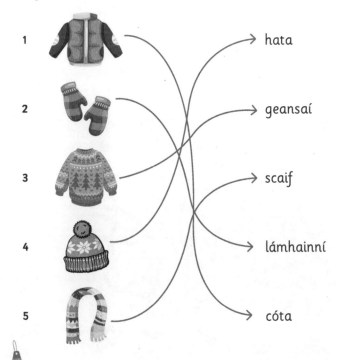

1
2
3
4
5

hata
geansaí
scaif
lámhainní
cóta

Page 70 Word Search

N	N	M	G	O	P	E	B	W	M	S	S	P	O	L	E	J	D
R	K	Z	V	I	X	E	N	D	I	H	C	L	C	X	N	Z	P
B	L	I	T	Z	E	N	H	A	P	T	L	I	C	T	O	N	H
Q	M	A	V	D	R	R	D	S	H	R	L	L	Q	O	Q	C	T
D	U	Z	J	O	U	K	N	H	X	N	A	O	Y	O	K	G	B
U	H	C	M	N	D	D	I	E	L	A	L	N	L	H	I	O	Y
B	R	L	O	N	O	C	U	R	C	G	R	W	C	M	R	Z	M
R	W	B	I	E	L	C	O	M	E	T	F	I	N	E	U	N	W
C	M	O	G	R	P	X	B	Q	K	J	T	K	U	L	R	Q	J
K	S	H	L	S	H	H	M	C	U	P	I	D	Z	O	N	E	X
L	O	H	X	E	M	L	J	O	O	G	I	T	D	P	V	U	Q
L	M	C	P	D	A	N	C	E	R	S	C	W	G	P	A	X	Z

Page 73 Sudoku

4	1	3	2
3	2	1	4
2	3	4	1
1	4	2	3

6	8	5	7
5	7	8	6
8	6	7	5
7	5	6	8

Page 74 Figure It Out!

The hot chocolate will cost €2.90. The cookies will cost €6. She will get €8 change. Each child received €5.

Page 75 Puzzle It Out